I0840920

LIBERAL SHOVE-DOWNS

Karen Kellock Ph.D.

Manual for Superior Men

This is a complete theory based on Einstein physics,
Political Psychology, Systems Theory
and Archetypal Psychiatry.

FORMULA

All success attraction
All disease obstruction
All recovery elimination

You must fast on all three

OBSTRUCTIONS:

People
Habit
Food

LIBERAL SHOVE-DOWNS

Invaded by hippies I felt crazy as I learned about boundaries. Hurtful name calling and criticism from jealousy: a dark force thru the centuries. Longwinded narcissists think their every word is gold when just by their loquacity it's all bull.   The past was stupid people who hated you and as stupid people do they got cruel too.   They project inadequacies/insecurities onto a child who then goes crazy and wild. Sins are mal-adaptive coping devices: crutches, mood elevators, anything making this pain cease.

BENEFITS OF NOT LOOKING BACK

MEMORY KEEPS US BACK
RELIVING IT TO CORRECT IT
THE STORY OF JOSEPH
GOD TURNS DRY PLACES FERTILE
FREE OF ALL LIMITATIONS
DISEASES AND DEBTS ARE GONE
YOU MUST GO FORWARD NOW
BAD MEMORIES ARE LITTLE GREMLINS
SEEKING PEOPLE FOR RELEASE
EXPECT REJECTION WHEN YOU INCREASE
THE GOD-CHOSEN LONER
FEELING AWKWARD BEING ALONE
NOT COMPELLED TO "STAY IN TOUCH"
LONERS HATE SOCIAL EVENTS
YOU ENJOY TRAVELING SOLO
IT'S MUCH EASIER BEING ALONE
ENVY WITHOUT UNDERSTANDING
THEY DON'T UNDERSTAND YOUR BURDENS
YOU HAD TO BE ISOLATED
WORKAHOLISM BLOCKS INSIGHT
THE CAMOUFLAGED FAST

BENEFITS OF NOT LOOKING BACK

MEMORY KEEPS US BACK

Seeing the pains & injustices of the past prevents us from seeing new favor. Forget em, you must sir.

Do **NOT** remember the former things or consider the things of old. I will do a new thing, behold. Isiah

A rear view mirror is good for checking the road but if we focus only on it we veer off course and crash it.

Keeping our eyes on the road ahead is essential to reach the destination. Not looking back son.

God calls us to leave the past behind and instead look forward with hope and confidence, aye.

RELIVING IT TO CORRECT IT

I kept reliving the past to correct it. How stupid! It only made it mad and blocked the future I wanted.

The pains & injustices should not hold us back but make us trust God since He solved it: fact.

Did not God solve an insolvable situation? He created a miracle so build faith from those solutions.

By forgetting the past we create a SPACE for the new blessings He has prepared, so do it now ok.

God promises renewal and restoration so look forward to that, forgetting the treachery of the past.

THE STORY OF JOSEPH

BENEFITS OF NOT LOOKING BACK

Joseph was betrayed by his own brothers, driven by envy. They even tried selling him into slavery.

He faced false accusations and unjust imprisonment feeling deep pain, betrayal and disappointment.

Despite these pains Joseph trusted God and this was rewarded as he shot up to leadership granted.

He forgave them who "meant evil against me but God meant it for good". That's the past, understood.

Joseph's story is a testament of how God can turn ashes into beauty so forget the past see.

That's how God acts in our lives in the **PRESENT**, creating rivers in the desert/all things pleasant.

GOD TURNS DRY PLACES FERTILE

God turns dry places into fertile ones if we can just stop reliving the past which was horrible/no fun.

Joseph went from being a slave to a ruler and his hardships saved many lives, so have no fear.

God was working in Joseph's life every moment, preparing him for that glorious future, amen?

Give all betrayal and hurt to God for He promises to create something new from it: **SUCCESS!**

God is working in our lives now, turning dry places into fertile land. Look forward & let Him do it then.

By trusting God and His plan, we can experience the beauty he brings in exchange for ashes man.

FREE OF ALL LIMITATIONS

BENEFITS OF NOT LOOKING BACK

If you trust God now He will free you of all curses, addictions and limitations from past ones.

He will free you of misery, poverty & depression. These all go when we trust God, it's our salvation.

This new thing will be better than any previous victory. Things always get better in God's kingdom see.

Change your focus and stop looking back. Staying in the review mirror can get you killed: fact.

This is a NEW DAY and God is doing something great and beautiful. Receive and claim this in full.

Now you'll see great favors: freed from captivity and abusive relationships, just as He did for me.

DISEASES AND DEBTS ARE GONE

Diseases, debts and oppressions will all now be gone. These are part of the promises as we go along.

You will live in abundance and prosperity in all areas of life. What a relief from the misery and strife!

This promise is ALL from letting the awful past go. This was Paul's biggest accomplishment you know.

Practice taking every thought captive. When it pops up, compartmentalize it and then get active.

Satan brings up the past in mind to hold you back. God doesn't want that cuz you're pure again: fact.

You're pure--white as snow--so why should you cringe over filthy incidents in the past when low?

My goodness, these people are dead, gone or toothless and you're still brimming with anger over this?

BENEFITS OF NOT LOOKING BACK

YOU MUST GO FORWARD NOW

You've got to go forward now: realize who's behind bad memories keeping you low, it's Satan ya' know.

Tho' you live in a mansion you're **CREATING** your hostile environment by going back so stop it hon'.

Memories are connected to bad habits: The more we give in to it the more they pop up, so stop it.

You must actively bless each day, knowing **YOU** create your reality and Satan wants to block it ok.

NEVER be a prisoner of your own thoughts. You must take thoughts **CAPTIVE** then urgently block.

BAD MEMORIES ARE LITTLE GREMLINS

Bad thoughts and memories are like little gremlins ok: see them as invaders and kill em right away.

See your mind as a **BATTLEGROUND** and shoot em down: every bad thought coming around.

As long as you cringe at memories you're a victim of Satan. I held myself down for decades man.

I tarnished my own self-image more than my enemies did, by allowing thoughts in that blighted.

You gotta stay high man. You gotta nourish your self-image to be in line with God's perception.

Take it as a daily exercise: to **NOTICE** and work on your thoughts that aren't created but stream by.

Satan says: "she's too happy, let's drop a bad thought in to keep her down and cringing in her lunacy".

SEEKING PEOPLE FOR RELEASE

BENEFITS OF NOT LOOKING BACK

Cringing in embarrassment, I'd let bad people in thinking I needed admiration to get me out of it.

If you're high and happy you get BUSY creating but if you're low feeling crappy you stop focusing.

It's more important than physical exercise: to keep your mind pure and high you must EXORCISE.

Spiritual attacks are usually envy. The devil is jealous and competition drives the evil in people see.

EXPECT REJECTION WHEN YOU INCREASE

When you increase in riches and get the new house they won't be around. It's just the way it is hon'.

When they attack, you fall back down into bad memories to confirm their dislike: don't do that.

God says you are holy and blameless in His sight. So why let these bad thoughts creep in, aye?

In the bible rulers and kings weren't even chosen. You must stop thoughts about petty competition.

Being chosen has nothing to do with status or popularity but belonging to God, a rarity.

THE GOD-CHOSEN LONER

Chosens have deeper relationships with themselves and their pets than with other humans.

You don't need to be validated or have constant company to share thoughts with [time wasted].

Being a "loner" carries bad connotations but it indicates you're of higher intelligence and a good one.

BENEFITS OF NOT LOOKING BACK

Being "outgoing" or having "connections" is seen as a good thing but I could never be that way see.

A loner likes to do most things by himself. It's the kid in class who wanted to walk alone like an elf.

A loner always avoids group activities and projects. He sits alone though seen as a hideous reject.

Being alone gives you perspective on things and get organized. What you enjoy, they despise.

FEELING AWKWARD BEING ALONE

Most people feel awkward or embarrassed being seen alone but you feel relaxed and free going solo.

The loner isn't glued to his smartphone. He doesn't need instant gratification just being alone.

The loner despises pointless phone calls and tiresome text messages. That brings hate from stooges.

The loner doesn't send texts or messages unless necessary so the phone is useless to him see.

You're outa reach for long periods at times. It used to bother em but now they know you're not social, aye.

NOT COMPELLED TO "STAY IN TOUCH"

You just don't feel compelled to constantly stay in touch. Are you a hater or just out to lunch?

Learning things and creating stuff is much more useful than catching up on the latest gossip fluff.

The loner prefers to work as a freelancer not a team player, for why add other annoying layers?

BENEFITS OF NOT LOOKING BACK

There is nothing more tedious to you than working with a buncha people. "Compromise" seems evil.

Working 9 to 5 seems too rigid, living by pointless rules. Let alone office parties and smiling at fools.

The loner does his best work alone where he's in charge of the schedule with 100% creative control.

LONERS HATE SOCIAL EVENTS

The loner hates social events. Why spend holidays with a buncha drunks when you could be alone in bliss?

He sees social events as something that eats up his time: something he values so greatly, aye.

The loner won't waste precious time on things he doesn't enjoy doing so he refuses to, aye.

This doesn't mean he hates hanging out with his friends, just that he wants it to be meaningful, amen!

It gets to where your headphones are your armor, just so they won't talk to you and waste time more.

I wasn't even listening to music most of the time, just wanting to keep strangers at bay, aye!

Having friends is nice but not at the expanse of your personal space so you instruct them to stay away.

You hate others meddling in your life and stay away from drama or the irrational, it's just strife.

YOU ENJOY TRAVELING SOLO

You enjoy traveling solo. Other people are just an encumbrance, you love enjoying it all alone.

BENEFITS OF NOT LOOKING BACK

Traveling with others has downfalls. You always gotta adapt to one who complains or hates it all.

Here you paid for this trip but now must compromise? You don't see why you should do that, aye.

IT'S MUCH EASIER BEING ALONE

It's so much easier just doing things on your own and in your way. Freedom is exhilarating, not groups ok.

I'm happiest alone, peaceful and content. The whole day is bliss but when someone arrives I lament.

You should feel no pressure to impress or compromise no matter at home or in a foreign land, aye.

Live your life as you please and remain unconcerned what others might think: that's happy see.

Your choices reflect your genuine SELF. Every minute your own and highly creative, the magic elf.

This is true independence. Unlike most people you wanna reflect, organize and set goals sis.

Stop worrying about looking cool or impressing people with your lifestyle. Jump ahead of rank and file.

t's not easy being a loner but once there you wouldn't change for the world, full of time wasting care.

We've a right to be who we are see. If you're happy with your life there's no need to change a thing.

ENVY WITHOUT UNDERSTANDING

Envy: they see your success not effort, your strength not wounds, your blessings not the burdens.

BENEFITS OF NOT LOOKING BACK

The covet the results of your hard work but could never handle the journey it took to get there first.

They envy the surface but remain forever ignorant of the depth, resilience and fortitude it took sis.

You were forged in fires unseen and shaped by challenges that would break those who envy see.

You faced trials that weren't just difficult but relentless, testing your core before coming to success.

THEY DON'T UNDERSTAND YOUR BURDENS

The burden you bore can't be understood by the crowd but by you alone, a test for you by the Lord.

Unique challenges tailored to purpose: Others faced a gust of wind while you were ripped apart by them.

Tested by betrayal, abandonment, being misunderstood or the waves of opposition tho' you were good.

Those who envy your success would have drowned in these obstacles for they have lesser wills.

Gold is made in the fire. To burn out the dross and anything else breakable to make you invincible.

Could your envious detractors have withstood that? Never, yet now they're more jealous than ever.

YOU HAD TO BE ISOLATED

You HAD to be isolated see, to be separated from forces seeking to diminish you and what you'd achieve.

You look simple now, a child again after going thru bedlam but you're just "blessed" it seems to them.

BENEFITS OF NOT LOOKING BACK

Pain wasn't just an adversary but the CHISEL that carved out your resilience & your brilliance.

Hardship wasn't your punishment but the honing stone making you sharp, precise and prepared friend.

The same setbacks making them crumble made you rise! That's resilience marking the chosen guys.

You're not just surviving but being sharpened, refined and polished by adversity, even treachery.

You met the path of endurance and became strong but they see you as calm, unaware of your storms.

They see you the calm giant and think your path was smooth, unaware of all you endured by fools.

The path was circuitous: you didn't plan how to get to heaven but you surely had to endure it sis.

The devil holds you bound by [1] making the event happen then [2] making you recall it often.

WORKAHOLISM BLOCKS INSIGHT

It's a funny thing but movies organize my thoughts by getting AWAY from the noisy crowd & chaos.

If a workaholic you gotta take a break BEFORE tired. You work in spurts but then relax & retire.

Not-working [relaxing] is when you get your insights. It's very important to stop-work & go light.

It's peculiar how watching movies saves time. Otherwise I'm susceptible to fretting over nothing.

If you're in a SPURT and get a lot done one day, relaxing the next is entirely logical, effective and ok.

BENEFITS OF NOT LOOKING BACK

Relaxing [letting tension, tunnel vision & active focus down] is essential for progress: then you've won.

You may work day and night without a break. Then you take a vaca: you **MUST** for your life's at stake.

You can overexert and be so tired: if you keep working you'll wish you hadn't for it ends uninspired.

You eat, you don't-eat. You work, you don't-work. Life's in **TWO** speeds: it's the week then rest is first.

If you're tired and uninspired then you don't work. You owe it to your purpose to relax or it's a curse.

God's man: don't work/relax. You must to fulfill your high purpose. Workaholism is a high tax.

THE CAMOUFLAGED FAST

Is it a camouflaged fast: almond butter, applesauce & raisins? Yes if you've been eating denser rations.

ATTACHMENTS & DERANGEMENTS

BOUNDARIES OR CRY CONSTANTLY
WITH BREAKTHROUGH LIFE CHANGES
THE RELEASE OF OBSTRUCTION
IT'S GOD SPIRIT IN THE CHOSEN
THE CHOSEN RELATE TO ANIMALS
FRUSTRATING DELAYS
FIND A NICE MAN BY FORGETTING
SINFUL DEVICES FOR SOLACE
LIVING WITH AN ALCOHOLIC
OVERCOMING IMMATURE FRIENDS
DON'T LET DECADES GO BY IN A FOG
REST BEFORE RULE
HOW LIBERAL FEMALES ARGUE [HARRIS]
GETTING MAUDLIN IS OFTEN FAKIN'
SMEARING YOU FOR DEMEANING
SUPERIOR FOR BEING POPULAR
THE COLLECTIVE DIS
THE DIFFERENT ACCUSED OF PERVERSION
USERS RAIN ON YOUR PARADE
FOOD THOUGHTS & FASTING A LOT

ATTACHMENTS & DERANGEMENTS

BOUNDARIES OR CRY CONSTANTLY

You could never have developed strong boundaries if they had not bothered you constantly.

Prosperity comes when totally relieved of unnecessary attachments and all emotional baggage.

I was relieved of attachments but carried em around in memories & intrusive thoughts: baggage.

I had to learn to stop thoughts and control my mind or be kept from what was destined to be mine.

It was as if my treacherous frenemies were living with me as I thought of em all day & night see.

WITH BREAKTHROUGH LIFE CHANGES

With breakthrough life changes very fast but you can't have that if stuck in the horrible past.

I had to make a choice: destiny and prosperity or stuck in the mud thinking about the past & enemy.

Let it be prosperity making you control mind for it's a clear choice: stop thoughts or stay poor, aye.

Keep looking AHEAD when intrusive thoughts keep you angry: choose destiny & a big payoff instead.

It was almost like I was addicted to my own adrenalin. Looking back to correct it is an addiction.

THE RELEASE OF OBSTRUCTION

ATTACHMENTS & DERANGEMENTS

The formula: All disease is obstruction, all recovery is ELIMINATION and then all success is attraction!

The **RELEASE OF OBSTRUCTION** acts as a suction cup to all you deserve as your destiny is freed up.

Your rise to fame wasn't a fluke or stroke of luck but who you were intended to be, so look up.

Seeing you're chosen for this task your appearance suddenly changes as in God's spirit you bask.

In a world obsessed with looking young you really **DO** look much younger than your age: what fun.

IT'S GOD SPIRIT IN THE CHOSEN

It's God's spirit revving you up with energy and spirit. It changes how you look and the others fear it.

Stop going back into the fight and your spirit rises, lighter than air, propelled by God's power.

People problems were put there to build social muscle not to obsess on forever in a constant tussle.

Prosperity doesn't approach it accelerates towards you, attracted by your undeniable magnetism too.

It's as if the universe recognizes the shift within you, your alignment with success in full view!

Friendship is like a diamond: it's rare, expensive and there are a lot of fakes so beware of flakes.

THE CHOSEN RELATE TO ANIMALS

The chosen ones relate more to animals than people: not human society but the cosmic natural.

ATTACHMENTS & DERANGEMENTS

Einstein: "all delays are the fastest route". It's God's timing: its explosion when your time comes up.

Frustrating delay builds character just as everything else negative. Accept it and even revel in it.

When old friends or relatives leave your side take is as another "assured success soon" sign.

It's part of the "success process" when old associates flake away. Let em go and praise God I say.

Learning to see all negative as positive is what builds the character of the chosen ones, so do it.

Cinderella is an archetype: the two wicked sisters made her so humble she attracted the right guy.

FRUSTRATING DELAYS

Frustrating delay is our last test. See it as God's edict to rest. Rest before rule then bask in success.

What a dangerous day when truth is called "reckless rhetoric" and the chosen are up a creek for it.

Your worth is not defined by those who refused to see it but by your God-created unstoppable spirit.

God has bigger plans for you than to be with those who never valued you in the first place Sue.

The awful past is behind you and the future is calling. Keep moving forward & forget em all darling.

The socially adapted probably aren't chosen since the latter relates to God not people devotion.

It takes a long time to get over it. The way they treat the chosen is cruel but God will vindicate it.

ATTACHMENTS & DERANGEMENTS

It still hurts decades later. It's how they treat the chosen but recall how they treated the savior.

Mistaking sex for love is the weak woman's biggest problem and a big cringe later after agin'.

FIND A NICE MAN BY FORGETTING

Finding a nice man and marrying won't be hard if you repent and pray for your total forgetting.

I shudder years later, long after persecutors are dead. It helps recalling what Jesus endured instead.

If you're set apart for God this is the territory. Being persecuted reflect Jesus in all His glory.

It hurts when your biggest persecutor was your mother. But that also is classic for sisters & brothers.

It's relieving for saints to see the patterns in the universe. If set apart by God the people curse!

Now just wait for your destiny to arrive. Your name's in the book & you're marked for prosperity, aye.

You overcame so much your character is like armour and the past is over, now you're the leader.

SINFUL DEVICES FOR SOLACE

You used sinful devices out of needing solace. Many saints had addictions they had to resolve.

Many women escaped into lecherous arms out of desperate need for love but now rise above.

Acceptance of prevalent sins comes from social hypnotism but the saints have all overcome.

ATTACHMENTS & DERANGEMENTS

It's pathetic the need for approval letting a man in. Save your self and privacy: a message to all women.

Accept in your heart that a lecher doesn't love you. All men want sex: this shouldn't be enigma sis.

LIVING WITH AN ALCOHOLIC

You've been living with the devil since the conduit is alcohol which Satan uses to ruin you doll.

Accept that the alcoholic is not himself. It's Satan coming up to you through an empty shell.

Anyone overcoming the Wife of the Alcoholic Syndrome is battle hardened with an armor of iron.

Neurophysiologically the alcoholic is out of control the minute he relapses back into his old hole.

Social hypnotism is fascism and the stupid cruelty coming from it explains all of history, amen.

All heroes had canyons cuz how else could they build muscle against em? Earlier I trusted everyone.

New age liberals say "it's all good". The earth is Satan's and they have much to learn, understood?

OVERCOMING IMMATURE FRIENDS

You've overcome so much from immature friends you're ready to rule and God is proud, amen.

It's classic narcissism to love you at first then devalue & discard suddenly. Go slow with people honey.

How things have changed from the good ol' days when mom's weren't jealous of their daughters ok.

ATTACHMENTS & DERANGEMENTS

Any daughter survivor should find surrogates in older women or even finding a good husband.

Many geniuses die of alcohol or drugs. Being outcasted they use such coping devices and go nuts.

Social hall religion struck terror in me. Knowing the Lord I knew it wasn't true and heavy in treachery.

DON'T LET DECADES GO BY IN A FOG

Don't be like me when decades went by in a fog. Catch this early and do something create for us all.

The chosen ones overcome adversity and the outcome is EMPATHY. Use it when re-involving socially.

Due to a trusting innocent spirit you were scammed & robbed but now they must face God's rod.

A fool is easily separated from his money but luckily because of that you became shrewd honey.

Let scammers be your best teachers. You need to use your money for good ends now and forever.

People need money and they're gonna seek yours. You gotta be a good steward now boys and girls.

Get rid of barnacles & parasites. Clean the ship of clutter & unnecessary stress for success, aye.

REST BEFORE RULE

REST BEFORE RULE. After your good work you must rest though friends are impatient fools.

Frenemies boast of being "well connected" but that's all a fake trip. The chosen are alone, that's it.

ATTACHMENTS & DERANGEMENTS

The mob so exhausts the spirit you'll do anything to escape it. Find a cabin or relocate quick.

It's the false accusations that are most debilitating and aggravating but it's classic so be preparing.

Even if not sinning you'll still be misfitting but see it as a mark of superiority and soon to be winning.

HOW LIBERAL FEMALES ARGUE [HARRIS]

She draws emptiness out combining mean smears. Instead of short snappy answers she filibusters.

She draws out empty answers to prevent any interruption by the other: that's the liberal sir.

She fills her time up with silly things then says "I'm speaking" when logic intervenes.

She speaks very slowly on stupid clichés so boring and that is the liberal female speaking.

In one contradiction after another she will frustrate with vacuous answers and yet another filibuster.

She is purely empty but spouts it arrogantly. It makes ya wanna hit her for her upstart treachery.

She bases her absurd assertions on what someone SAID not logic, that's how they all do it.

There is no integrating paradigm to her logic, it's all platitudes & hearsay of one without credit.

SHE GETS MAUDLIN BUT IT'S FAKIN'

She gets maudlin with tears over the results of her actions while blaming the opponent for em.

ATTACHMENTS & DERANGEMENTS

The mob so exhausts the spirit you'll do anything to escape it. Find a cabin or relocate quick.

It's the false accusations that are most debilitating and aggravating but it's classic so be preparing.

Even if not sinning you'll still be misfitting but see it as a mark of superiority and soon to be winning.

HOW LIBERAL FEMALES ARGUE [HARRIS]

She draws emptiness out with opponent smears. Instead of short snappy answers she filibusters.

She draws out empty answers to prevent any interruption of the other: that's the liberal sir.

She fills her time up with empty answers and says "I'm speaking" when logic intervenes, then slurs.

She speaks very slowly drawing out her platitudes so boring and that is the liberal female's speaking.

In one contradiction after another she will frustrate with empty answers and one boring filibuster.

She is purely empty but spouts it arrogantly. It makes ya wanna hit her for her upstart treachery.

She bases her absurd assertions on what someone SAID not logic, that's how they all do it.

There is no integrating paradigm to her logic, it's all platitudes & hearsay of one without credit.

GETTING MAUDLIN IS OFTEN FAKIN'

She gets maudlin with tears over the results of her actions while blaming the opponent for em.

ATTACHMENTS & DERANGEMENTS

It's all an act with empty platitudes filling in the gaps while preventing the other to ever interject.

She smiles as she wields her deceptive knife but comes unhinged when the other reveals her strife.

She wants to "turn the page" with a "new brand of leadership" tho' that turned everything to shit.

SMEARING YOU FOR DEMEANING

She smears the opponent for "demeaning" others while she demeans him constantly with her covers.

She brings up non-issues and expands them out too. It's so frustrating debating a liberal "cool".

When you try to interrupt her filibuster she castigates you as just another brutal male interrupter.

She is intellectually lazy, relying on her contacts, status, gender, connections, image or whatever.

She derides the other by what others say about him while she has social connections, amen?

She bloviates about her great influence or elite mentors like as if that means everything as a debater.

Protected by her entourage she figures whatever word salad she throws out will be sufficient sir.

SUPERIOR FOR BEING POPULAR

She's superior because she's popular and connected: he's inferior cuz he's seen as lunatic or hated.

It's so hard to move on. Just when you feel bliss, the awful past comes in like a hurricane to dis.

ATTACHMENTS & DERANGEMENTS

Just when happy the past hits like a ton of bricks. That's what it's like being owned like this.

Watch out for the vicious old witch. Don't fool yourself about these bad archetypes, they exist.

THE COLLECTIVE DIS

Any chosen knows about persecution: it's pure projection outa their limited understanding son.

The limited hear something about you and fill their cups with it. Think of Trump, the greatest victim blitz.

Especially if in a small town, news travels fast and they want to believe the worst about the renown.

The greater you are the more limited their understanding of a star who is targeted from afar.

You can be innocent and harmless and the herd will do this. I have experienced it: a collective DIS.

It's coming from THEIR limited minds & perceptive system, not from anything wrong with you son.

Persecution for no reason is just something you gotta get thru but it will toughen you for later Sue.

Hurt: they hate your guts when you did nothing wrong, accused of disgusting things by the throng.

THE DIFFERENT ACCUSED OF PERVERSION

The more different [renowned] the more accused of things like perversion, all from their own projection.

If the past hits like a ton of bricks what is the answer sis? The one & only solution is forgiveness.

ATTACHMENTS & DERANGEMENTS

If you're one of the greats you WILL be persecuted see. Jesus said "they will hate you as they hated me."

You're still angry so you WANNA go back and fight it out. But you can't cuz they're dead so forget it all.

Users are just comin' over to do what you do. You spend a mint on pleasures and they want some too.

Be smart. SPEND a mint on pleasure but watch carefully who comes over and draw boundaries sir.

USERS RAIN ON YOUR PARADE

Let users in and they'll inevitably rain on your parade. It's a subconscious thing with bad spirits ok.

If you're gonna live high on the hog that's ok with God unless you let His hedge down, that's all.

99% of your problems came from people involvements. You'll push forward fast if you can face this.

FOOD THOUGHTS & FASTING A LOT

Four tacos [with 5" corn tortillas] and two tabs. of almond butter is 33 carbs for the day sir.

The lower the carb the lower the antioxidants. I'm not giving up my apple sauce for instance.

I don't go for "lowcarb veggies" but wonderful fruits so my daily carbs are <100 to stay fit & cute.

I was obsessed in keeping carbs low [<30} until I saw how much better I felt with fruits ya know.

I used to enjoy buttered popcorn but now it causes acid reflux all day and joint pain the next morn.

ATTACHMENTS & DERANGEMENTS

Things keep changing as we age. You just have to micro-evolve with diet to stay all the rage.

It's the KIND of food that affects, not calories etc. Today I'm having just fruit, so good for ya.

Pineapple and almond butter: what a delicious lunch and it revs up my energy so much better.

SPIRITUAL AWAKENINGS
vs. Liberal Shovedowns

RELATIONAL IMPASSES
NO CHANCE IN RESOLVING IT
RELATIONSHIPS DISPERSE
RE-EVALUATION OF BELIEF SYSTEMS
SO THAT'S THAT!
BURSTING INTUITION
NO MORE NORMAL CONVERSATIONS
PEOPLE PROBLEMS TAUGHT US
READ PSALMS ABOUT TREACHERY
YOU'RE GONNA FEEL ALONE
THE NARCISSISTS
ALONE BEFORE THE THRONE
HEALTH ADVICE FOR SPIRIT
START WITH FRUIT
HIGH FAT FRUIT/VEGGIE DIET

SPIRITUAL AWAKENINGS
vs. Liberal Shovedowns

RELATIONAL IMPASSES

Relationships reach impasses where you can't even talk. It's so sad we can't accept it at all.

You've reached an impasse and trying to make em see things your way won't help in this mess.

People have different perceptions. Agreeing to disagree allows you to STOP and move forward son.

Holding a grudge won't help. Either accept the disagreement [put on a shelf] or get out.

If you wanna stay you'll have to let it go. It's an issue that will tear you apart you know.

NO CHANCE IN RESOLVING IT

You wanna keep bringing it up to iron it out. It's a matter of respect/wanting resolution, but give up.

Two choices in this: Either bury it, go forward and give up resolving it or leave the relationship.

This irresoluble issue could signal your spiritual awakening. It happens from mentally separating.

With spiritual awakening your relationships begin to shift. Traumatic things happen, expect it.

You'll see that after the toughest times of life, that's when spiritual awakenings happen, aye.

SPIRITUAL AWAKENINGS

There's no doubt about it, all will change. Crazy turn of events outa the blue, even the deranged.

Irrational things you can't explain, tough times of losses, no gains. These things will wake you up ok.

Spiritual awakenings wake you up to the realities of life & relationships so they don't hurt like that.

RELATIONSHIPS DISPERSE

You will lose a lot of people as relationships shift drastically. You're left alone practically.

The way you see your own family, reality or longtime friends changes from your earlier ages.

You see reality now not the shovedowns from a fogged brain. It's quite a wake up and shattering.

You were naive and mollifying just to get along but in reaching this impasse your mind is open.

You start to understand things: "this is what it is". You recall friends' warnings earlier dismissed.

Your dreams at night will become more vivid. Like a friend parking on your lawn being livid.

RE-EVALUATION OF BELIEF SYSTEMS

You are re-evaluating your own belief system. That's what's happening after a shovedown.

What you think and how you see people change. You saw hairdressers as high status at that age.

People lose significance not just in station but what they thought then or ability to frighten.

SPIRITUAL AWAKENINGS

As you see anyone can do anything you make your own dreams a reality just as they lose standing.

You don't put people on pedestals. Even those doing amazing things they aren't a god you know.

You can do it to: You put the time in, the stars align and you're a star like them, so admired too.

You feel detached and disconnected from a spiritual awakening: to society, friends or family.

You see these things for what they are and don't even want connection with these falling stars.

SO THAT'S THAT!

So that's that: you don't even want connection cuz they're not what you want anyway son.

We gain more wisdom with time so your world cracks open and reveals the stale vs. the sublime.

Now your intuition goes thru the roof. You see thru things for what they are: a spiritual war.

If your friend is a raging lion but acts like he's not one you see thru his game and that's it son.

Your intuition does not lie. You've awoken and feel sick to your stomach sitting next to that guy.

You felt sick in the gut before about him but quickly dismissed it having bought the shovedown.

BURSTING INTUITION

Just looking at the picture of one you knew makes you feel their dark energy/how they were cruel.

SPIRITUAL AWAKENINGS

You see abusive spouse & don't fight it anymore. Acceptance brings reversal & your spirit soars.

You're sensitive to energies and separate from those guys. Now you don't fight to change em see.

You sense inauthenticity and manipulation: like how they irrationally become like roaring lions.

You know when they don't like you. Tho' you're quiet you have the loudest mind & they eschew.

NO MORE NORMAL CONVERSATIONS

You can't have normal conversations anymore. They fly off the handle as small minds will abhor.

You're quiet cuz most people haven't experienced what you have. You're diffident now: no sass.

They're still on that baseline level of delusion of what they want life to be like: better be careful.

They don't see reality for what it is but what they WANT it to be, buttressed by their friends & family.

You're now very hard to manipulate. You used to be an immature pushover in your earlier days.

Like insecure pampered women used to attracting men: you can suddenly see through all of em.

PEOPLE PROBLEMS TAUGHT US

So many bad experiences with people will eventually bring on this spiritual awakening re: evil.

It wakes up your spirit that is designed to protect you. God is moved raging against your foes too.

SPIRITUAL AWAKENINGS

As spirituality becomes more important everyday existence fades and people seem listless.

The way ew love nature & go on walks sensing eternity--that's what's important to you and me.

You're now connected to animals more, to silent prayer and reading God's word [no TV anymore].

You see how detrimental it was to neglect spirituality. To be part of the matrix & gossip especially.

You see how people fall away when you're in trouble. How they take your money & then double.

You see how frail relationships were, how they'd roar like a lion then make all nice, a fake cover.

How pathetic it was how they'd use you up then on the way down they could never be found, yup.

It's ironic how a spiritual awakening brings these sad realizations but that's how it is son.

READ PSALMS ABOUT TREACHERY

At this time read Psalms as it's all about the treachery of people rising up against you son.

You can't imagine drugging, partying & boozing like them. It's bad energy you escaped from, amen.

You cried out to God and He delivered you. This was a miracle you'll never forget, and you grew.

You cried out to God and they did not. God answered His children and treated them like rot!

Read the Psalms if you don't believe me. God is very prejudiced & delivers you from treachery.

SPIRITUAL AWAKENINGS

Awake, you'll see crazy synchronicities: magic coincidences reveal when free of treachery.

You're a changed person, a real adult sir. You want to be of service to others with a life that matters.

Things take time, your purpose takes time. It's when the roast is done and you can't hurry it up, aye.

YOU'RE GONNA FEEL ALONE

You're gonna feel alone while breaking those patterns. Of hate, envy or being hurt by life's turns.

Your mind's overloaded and everything's different. It's a hard time but look ahead to fulfillment.

You feel the world is coming to an end, and it IS. What you thought was real isn't and it's scary sis.

Life doesn't make sense anymore but suddenly you break through to a new world and reality.

So too on social media you'll find your life empty. It's all an archetype so you'd better be ready.

As old systems fall away just hang on/don't feel loneliness taking over, just look forward.

Don't even go to your email to check anymore. It's an addiction and you're waiting for far more.

THE NARCISSISTS

The narcissists had no problem abandoning you so silence is the best policy with them too.

If you can't get rid of em they will make your life a living hell. They will keep coming back even still.

SPIRITUAL AWAKENINGS

How many times have they discarded you and when they came back you welcomed them Sue?

They are evil, cunning and manipulative. They want in your head so you must silence them instead.

You couldn't accomplish your full potential surrounded by losers. That's why you're isolated now sir.

You never fit your environment and it hurt. God removed em [a curse] so you can come first.

You were meant for greatness and they wanted to stop that, knowing nothing but how to be rats.

ALONE BEFORE THE THRONE

So now you're alone but don't fret son for how else could you develop fully for the throne?

It was meant for you to not fit in for you had a bigger calling. But it sure hurt at the beginning.

It was meant for you to stand out but that also triggered resentment when you showed clout.

You don't want em thinking they even have a chance. That's over or you'll be back in that evil dance.

Having had a spiritual awakening they're gonna want you back. Do that and your world turns black.

Their mask slipped and you saw who they were. That was the day you resumed your destiny sir.

These are toxic people, not team players. They do nothing to benefit you, they only want favors.

His mask slipped and you saw reality. He's a raging lion telling us he's not and you felt it sweetie.

SPIRITUAL AWAKENINGS

HEALTH ADVICE FOR SPIRIT

As you break thru you experience fatigue and brain fog. It's inevitable with a brain shift to God's law.

Know when to rest: when to take an hour nap, a warm bath or anything else which releases stress.

Recharge with liquids, healthy nutrition or a happy day cooking: any way to get God's vitaminerals in.

Eat fruit but mostly vegetables to clean the bowels out. You've been in sick systems and are blocked.

Eat meat if you wish but we're not all meat-eaters you know. Find your best diet and do it now.

START WITH FRUIT

Start with fruit then raw/steamed vegetables for lunch. Use butter & cheese: stay thin/go French.

Butter, cream or cheese in your veg dishes will elevate glucagon and keep you satiated son.

Leave off the starch if you wanna be fast, thin, cute and quick. Even spuds make me feel stuck.

Use fat not starch & you'll see what I mean. The French are high-fat but thin like most Europeans.

Vegetables will broom out the intestines and this cleanliness will show on your carved face.

Cheekbones and all features will now show. Not the bloated planes like most Americans you know.

HIGH FAT FRUIT/VEGGIE DIET

With a high-fat fruit & veggie diet you'll be clear, energetic and quick: a goodlookin' guy or chick.

SPIRITUAL AWAKENINGS

Clarify your diet and you'll be on your way. It's the last piece of the puzzle for work even fame.

For details on the high-fat vegetarian diet read Champion Guides by Dr. Karen Kellock, aye.

You need fat for the brain, glands and skin. A porcelain glow will be yours along with distinct features.

We're not all meat-eaters. After having fish I wake up the next morning a little depressed/blurred.

But dairy--cream, butter or cheese sauces--are perfect and light, making meals so delicious/right.

If you want eggs, test it. That's ovo-vegetarian, cheese if lacto- and fish is rasta-, it's all legitimate.

I believe diet is crucial to success. If you want pancakes or fast food go ahead but you'll feel like lead.

Eat nuts for snacks, they're also high-fat and will keep you satiated and feeling no lack.

LIBERAL SHOVE-DOWNS

ALL IS COMPENSATORY
AVOID SELF-EXPLANATION MODE
GET PAST DREAMS OF BLISS
GENIUS KNOWS THE VALUE OF LEISURE
THE SUPPRESSED SELF
BREAKING TOXIC TIES
SOUL TIES ARE SEXUAL
LIBERALS: IT'S SIT DOWN, SHUT UP
UNWISE AND WICKED CRITICS
DON'T ENVY, THEY'RE DONE SEE
AVOIDING OLD TRIGGERS
WOMEN USE SMEAR CAMPAIGNS
SMEARING MENTAL ILLNESS
FEMINISM DESTROYS WOMEN
SINISTER DARK FORCE OF JEALOUSY
EX-SCAPEGOATS ARE BULLY-SLAYERS
TO MALICIOUSNESS, NO LOSS
BLACK SHEEP AND HOMEOSTASIS
CHILDREN WITH NO BOUNDARIES
FINDING THE NEW SCAPEGOAT
SCAPEGOAT MATE-SELECTION
DYSFUNCTIONAL FAMILY TRAITS
IT'S NOT WOMEN BUT THE SPIRIT IN EM
YOUTHFUL PASSIONS MISDIRECTED
UNDOING COLLEGE CULTURE
ADAPTING TO BEDLAM
WOMEN ARE JEALOUS
OVERCOMING TEMPTATION
KNOWING YOUR LIMITATIONS
TAKING ON MISJUDGMENTS TO BE LIKED

LIBERAL SHOVE-DOWNS

POLITICS OF IDENTITY: WHO I AM
UNREPORTED BLACK-ON-BLACK VIOLENCE
FRIGHTENING FEROCIOUS FEMINISTS
LOVING THE WHOLE WORLD OR SLUR
NON-BINARY IS ANTI-MALE
WOMEN'S RIGHTS AND ALL KINDS OF STUFF
PRO TENNIS CHANGES AS FEMINISM DERANGES IT
HEAVENLY HOME OR ANGRY FEMINIST SLUM?
PATHETICALLY INFANTILE BEHAVIOR IS V ALOR
WOMEN HOLD EACH OTHER DOWN
JOY AND LOVE NO MATTER THE FACTS
VIRTUE SIGNALING CREATES TRAGEDY
PULLING THE FEMALE CARD
HOSTILE INVASION OF YOUNG MEN
THE DEMENTED LEFT HELPS THE RICH
THE CRUELTY OF TRANSNATIONAL
MERKEL MADNESS SEEN AS FEMALE LOVINGNESS
LIBERALISM SUX CUZ IT HAS NO DISGUST
GOD LOVERS ARE GROUP HATERS
JUNK SCIENCE AND HISTORICAL REVISIONISM
NEO-CON GLOBALIST TROJAN HORSES
DON'T TELL ME THE LIBERAL NARRATIVE I REJECT IT
EQUALITY OF OUTCOME IS HORRIBLE
MERKEL MADNESS AND FEMALE ILLOGIC/VIRTUE SIGNALING
PEOPLE SEEN AS STATISTICS NOT RAW FACTS
WE'RE ON THE PATH OF SOUTH AFRICA
NASTINESS AND DISRESPECT
EQUAL RIGHTS VS. "EQUALITY OF OUTCOME"
MULTICULTURALISTS STONING RAPED WOMEN
MULTICULTURALISTS ACCEPT STONING RAPED WOMEN
YOUR SOLUTION: GET TO WORK--DISCOVERY!
DO THE WORK, DESERVE SUCCESS

LIBERAL SHOVE-DOWNS

Success like a Tsunami: A giant wave of frenetic activity just after nothing, zero, silence, apathy.

Why should you feel so ashamed. Your situation was virtuous compared to modern sluts & witches.

So you're a late bloomer, the best talents ripen late: those attracting souls to heaven's gate.

Because people are cruel & ageist remarks aren't cool you learn how to deal with/manage the people.

Easter. You've been hidden under God's hand. Is this the day He lifts it so you get some fans?

Their rejections spurred me on. There was no way I was gonna lose to them/their dream disparagin'.

ALL IS COMPENSATORY

Remember, everything is compensatory with the narcissist so if you reach out expect it sis.

The more they disparaged/rejected me the harder I worked. I didn't sink in my swill, a curse.

So you were sick, wasted, an embarrassment, a fool and a bum. This is all corrected by God hon'

So you failed miserably in front of the whole world to see. This is no big thing to Big Daddy.

A genius in the making didn't have time for rules and regulations so his early life was rocky.

LIBERAL SHOVE DOWNS

So what, Jesus saw it all and He was there. There isn't a sin He doesn't know of so cast your care.

Devil toyed with me since birth. I was born in hot water then it was all about overcoming the curse.

Narcissists are constantly in compensation mode serving inner strains, tensions and conflicts.

Narcs must demonstrate that you're the problem so they don't have to face the inner ones.

To prove this they trigger fights to show you as the unstable one--their favorite trick hon'

AVOID SELF-EXPLANATION MODE

What you think they deride so you go into explanation mode. When you do that growth is slowed.

The more you go into your justification the more they poke holes and the females just ghost.

The deeper/more frantic you dig to be right the more they fight until you've lost it, good night.

Don't justify self cuz you don't have to. Don't feel small cuz in the eyes of God all men start equal.

Must you justify yourself that strongly esp with one who isn't paying much attention to you anyway?

Bashed for independent thought: "gotta have everything your way huh?" What a mental clot.

"Where'd you learn to think like that" or "guess you don't care about anyone else" he spat.

Your insistence on being you and doing things your way they interpret as their insignificance ok.

LIBERAL SHOVE DOWNS

That's the way their operate: shame you for thinking like you do to quit being the problem ok.

They see you responsible for their moods. That's a problem since they're myopic & you're a tool.

He's perplexed so he says "do you realize the trouble you've created around here? Hex, smear.

Then you say "I didn't mean that" and he's got you going again--part of the game of narcissists.

They intimidate your boundaries. They're your identity so they bust them & invite flying monkeys.

Try to push thru your wise agenda and he says "you're not a team player" or "you're selfish"

They make having boundaries a bad thing and will call you neurotic so shut the door/ignore the ring.

It's not that you have a firm definition of self it's that you're a disruptive force and it's your fault.

GET PAST DREAMS OF BLISS

You have dreams of connubial bliss with a kiss but a guy like this can't be reached/doesn't care sis.

Since he can't introspect he can't solve inner conflicts and strains causing the compensation game.

Get rid of all that printers ink--books--which you never read and just display to impress the kooks.

Not working [relaxing] is very necessary so stop compulsing and enjoy the right-brain leisurely.

Though I realize I was insane I am still miffed about the smear campaigns by "concerned" claims.

LIBERAL SHOVE DOWNS

GENIUS KNOWS THE VALUE OF LEISURE

You're not wasting time when not-working. You're recharging so I have to force it [stopping].

Turn on the music, take a toke or whatever you have to do to SWITCH to life-extend using balance.

SWITCH to the right brain where all the magic is, the jigsaw puzzle fits, a cornucopia/no twits.

STOP girl, stop. Take a toke, put on the music, pet the dogs or run around the block but STOP.

For the gems--rich insights--are in the relaxation mode so you gotta switch to not miss the show.

Nothing compares to rich insights during leisure thus would-be genius has incapacity for leisure.

You've already proven yourself a thousand times over so don't get involved with a mental butcher.

I know it hurts [devalue/discard] and tends to addict you more but it's the last time, if you remember.

Falsehood is both tiring and boring. The truth is hell fire preaching and it's fascinating and relieving.

THE SUPPRESSED SELF

Living with a controller you suppress what you really feel and end up with anxiety, depression, feeling ill.

Living with a word tyrant you can become negative and cynical, never seeing the cause of it all.

Narcissists have to have an adversary. Go grey rock: start pulling back into your own reality.

LIBERAL SHOVE DOWNS

Ultimately when you begin to get SELF back you can clearly see that he never cared anyway.

BREAKING TOXIC TIES

Breaking unhealthy toxic ties to a person who means you no good but you long for: how to do it.

The addiction stronghold keeps rescue tips out and destructive thoughts in preventing changing.

It's so strong that despite prayer/study the attachment bond overwhelms any attempts at escape.

"You're not getting any younger" or "better keep your eye peeled for a husband" signals danger.

Trapped in relationships that are going nowhere: how to disentrench from the love addiction scare.

It's a Merry Go-Round: takes you on a fast & thrilling ride always ending in the same place: down.

It's a fast ride going nowhere. Around and around you go always thinking it's a new love launcher.

It's obdurate and hell getting out of it cuz it's a stronghold: nothing gets in/you can't get out.

Bible says to cast down imaginations: you're always visioning these fantasies so you pursue on.

Trapped in a relationship going nowhere, clear to everybody but the victim which is you sister.

There's a reason she keeps talking herself out of common sense: a stronghold is a heavy fence.

Unrealistic expectations are a set up to get hurt. But if we go by God's promises we can rest first.

LIBERAL SHOVE DOWNS

They asked why she was a success. She got involved with a nice man for a change she said.

She'd been promiscuous in her twenties and didn't know it--we swim in muddy waters then deny it.

SOUL TIES ARE SEXUAL

Stop thirsting for company and start clearing then watch all the mass attractions coming.

With any sex event you become ONE with them taking on their spirits creating an ugly appearance.

The. strongest man in the world was taken out by a sexual soul tie. Can you imagine that, aye.

Soul ties are sexual in nature. The only good soul tie is marriage, all the others become torture.

Wives of pastors caught with porn committing suicide: it's all from the ontologically fatal insight.

A man giving his power to the Delilah Spirit will soon wish he hadn't, falling into a pit for it.

The fatal insight in your ONTOLOGY is that your world is NOT what you thought it was/its sick.

You start out in a haze then with time it all fills in and you're amazed at how you were wrong ok.

Everything has an ending. Just as your time has come the foe starts to collapse and ends falling.

LIBERALS: IT'S SIT DOWN, SHUT UP

It's sit down, shut up--accept my view or you're out. Then I'll get everyone against you chump.

LIBERAL SHOVE DOWNS

They even take pride in being narcissistically entitled and selfish, it's our generational trash.

You gotta take people for who they are now not for how you hope they will change in the future.

Just focus on what God sees and you'll get so good you won't care what they think so stupidly.

You feel valueless and guilty for setting boundaries. These are signs of narcissistic frenemies.

Narcissists get away with what they do cuz there's always an enabler or sympathizer too.

UNWISE AND WICKED CRITICS

They don't know what they're talking about but you do now. Stand straight and tell the truth: wow!

They weren't born that way. It's all due to liberal feminism and its effect on the personality.

The progressives want dirty oil from international killers not clean oil from our drillers. Bill Hagerty

You have an enemy and like stink on stink he'll never give up and that's why you feel nuts.

I'm not mad at you anymore. I'm just so glad that I'm in my cozy home [here] and you're there.

The enemy assigns a Delilah to those of great purpose and destiny, to mess them up quickly.

Nothing you say has value/you're not that interesting. After being with them that's the feeling.

DON'T ENVY, THEY'RE DONE SEE

LIBERAL SHOVE DOWNS

Don't be envious of a foe spreading his wings because tomorrow he'll be cut down quickly.

Don't be envious as Jezebel rises up in beauty cuz it's an illusion preceding her fall from destiny.

Narcissists will build a harem around em to pick up the pieces allowing em zero accountability.

The more you try to impress me the more it turns me off. I can see right thru you haughty chump.

Having perfected, you have to give it now. The best talents ripen late, telling crowds of God.

He thinks he's so hot but he's not. The clear can see right through the nut who struts his stuff.

There are great women who made it thru the feminist haze and those who lived before hell ok?

They weren't born as bitches. It's all from feminism and divorcing men/God to be pagan witches.

I don't wanna witness brutal/strange customs in foreign countries and I don't wanna see you honey.

The tough feminist types are really mean and even intimidate men who avoid their scene.

AVOIDING OLD TRIGGERS

I thought that era was over now high as a kite and clever but talking to you I'm back in the gutter.

Even talking to a narcissist invalidates the true self and even disconfirms everything you thought.

Don't get crazy when people copy, you can't stamp that out honey just see it as a complement ok.

LIBERAL SHOVE DOWNS

People copy me constantly and I think: when I leave this earth this will be my legacy see.

For nothing stays the same and even your house could be gone, there is no security but in God.

The Jezebel spirit arises from a childhood unfortunate so it's very hard to deal with, know that.

Having come from a split [broken family] it causes a split for that's a comfort zone in the pits.

WOMEN USE SMEAR CAMPAIGNS

It was one smear campaign after another driving me under her. That's the story of my sister.

Your "help" was just opportunity to smear me all over town and like a fool I let you in my home.

Going no contact is keeping your mind, heart and soul intact cuz if wounded again you're dead.

Soft, gentle and tender--there's no more of that is there. It's such a cold climate I want my mother.

They even think they are supposed to be furious, mean, standing up for some weird something.

Were neighbors the enablers to the narcissist sadist calling himself a helper in his mental illness?

Just because he was a professional the neighbors took his side against his abused wife, aye.

SMEARING MENTAL ILLNESS

You smeared her mental illness so she spent 30 years in a blank fog reacting against the mob.

LIBERAL SHOVE DOWNS

They won't listen to an abused wife if her spouse is a professional: social hypnotism rules y'all.

You smeared my mental illness and I'm supposed to like this? You told the whole town outa concern sis?

If you don't understand this that's ok, there's plenty who do and this is directed to them today.

They falsely assume since they're a group vs. just you that they're right and you're a savage too.

She was the golden child and I was the black sheep and when that matrix took hold I went mad see.

I paid my dues, that I know. I was punished for sin like everyone on earth when reflecting below.

They were all coping strategies. Self-defeating coping devices when the gut signals treacheries.

Unforgiveness is carrying a boulder around. Give yourself a break cuz either way they've forgotten.

FEMINISM DESTROYS WOMEN

It wasn't so much **THEM** as it was what feminism does to women. They're a herd, a clique echoin'.

It was a long, dark, crooked path and very sad. Then He put me on the Potter's Wheel and here I am.

She used husband's alcoholism against friend as a weapon and it worked despite Al Anon.

Biden is deliberately tone deaf by being surrounded by those like himself as in a bubble or shell.

As far as your age, you were born for such a time as this when the youth are unaware/hypnotized.

LIBERAL SHOVE DOWNS

Thinking you're hot cuz you're on the coast, smoke dope and listen to reggae but go inland honey.

For energy: I won't give up my time, my home, my herb nor will I allow anything imposed on me.

Since sin keeps you longer than you thought it's good news with Jesus it's all wiped out.

SINISTER DARK FORCE OF JEALOUSY

This is the dark winter of antibody enhancement. We're constantly sick from inwardly fighting back.

The past: They were stupid people who hated you and as stupid people do they got cruel too.

Insight: The constant manipulations of childhood were a projection of a psychotically stunted parent.

They projected their inadequacies and insecurities onto this child who then went crazy and wild.

Hurtful name calling and criticism rooted in jealousy, a sinister and dark force thru the centuries.

Sins were mal-adaptive coping devices. Crutches, mood elevators, anything making pain cease.

Often we don't change 'til we hit bottom: when the price of the crutch is greater than the payoff.

EX-SCAPEGOATS ARE BULLY-SLAYERS

Whisperings in a small town reflect gossipings of an abusive sibling planting evil seeds see.

Those who've been thru the scapegoat role are extremely empathic because they know.

LIBERAL SHOVE DOWNS

Empathy was learned to keep in step with the narcissist's needs and now it's a precious gift see.

Ex-scapegoats become our rock stars: champions of the oppressed and empathic bully-slayers.

The scapegoat easily goes no contact with the family or origin, after all that they owe em nothing.

In most cases the scapegoat is gone for good, they don't re-unite and that's it studies showed.

All studies show that yes, the family does self-destruct after the scapegoat leaves, it's a fact.

Collapse, dysfunction or confusion: this is the state of the scapegoat system after expurgation.

BLACK SHEEP AND HOMEOSTASIS

When the black sheep leaves the toxic family unit if falls apart--that is how all these systems are.

The toxic family was never healthy despite the mobbing mentality bullying the ONE as the sickie.

The system was sick before the scapegoat was even born but they still think he's the problem.

The system NEEDS a scapegoat for narcissistic supply so in fear the flying monkeys pick fights.

The flying monkeys will do whatever they need to do to prove it's not them causing the problem.

When we study intergenerational trauma we see the problem was never the scapegoat momma.

Since the enablers stay, it goes on for generations and centuries before someone walks away.

LIBERAL SHOVE DOWNS

The flying monkeys are codependent with the narcissist in a destructive unhealthy relationship.

TO MALICIOUSNESS, NO LOSS

It's not a loss to lose family when they're malicious, vicious, vengeful people aiming to hurt.

It is not a loss to lose such abusive people. That insight alone can save you years of grief and trouble.

What a relief. You can finally be who you are destined to be. Sibling abuse has kept you unfree.

Flying monkeys have no compassion or empathy. They don't respect you, they're enemy territory.

Despite family closeness there's an elephant in the room of toxic abusive patterns of doom.

They don't love you or respect your boundaries. They're beholden to the narcissist not you honey.

CHILDREN WITH NO BOUNDARIES

Children caught in this setup were never taught healthy boundaries. They are invisible with no voice.

Being "invisible" they grow up lonely and isolated, unable to express the price of such hatred.

The third trait is jealousy . One becomes extremely envious and mean-spirited towards one see.

As siblings fear being the next one, and the scapegoat's gone, what we have is an imploded system.

A narcissist is going to get her supply one way or another so another monkey becomes loser.

LIBERAL SHOVE DOWNS

They are rotten to the core and will not change. Despite their image of goodness, good riddance.

The scapegoat being gone forever won't ever change the root of the toxic family or the future.

Once scapegoat # 1 is gone the intergenerational abuse cycle demands mobbing of scapegoat #2.

FINDING THE NEW SCAPEGOAT

They're gonna find a new scapegoat since intergenerational trauma maintains itself.

As soon as scapegoat #1 is no longer in the system the squabbling will go on, bickering full blown.

Scapegoat # 1 wins as he survives the toxic unit and lives to tell about it as the system falls apart.

Scapegoat: You won, you're free, this is something to celebrate. You overcame this block of pain.

No more living in these dynamics that are so psychologically abusive. Lunatics, elusive.

Have you been hell and back due to this intergenerational trauma? You're free now, hah!

The scapegoat is the predominant role in the family system as he gets the wrath of the narcissist.

This scapegoat is impacted most by constant mental health attacks. An entire childhood, wrecked.

Scapegoat has chronic depression as well as an ongoing state of self-doubt and blame, saddened.

SCAPEGOAT MATE-SELECTION

LIBERAL SHOVE DOWNS

The scapegoat then chooses partners who replicate all of these invalidation cycles of childhood.

People who've been scapegoated are so empathic they're the best red flag detectors as adults.

Being scapegoated by a group is a traumatic experience lasting a lifetime in emotional collapse.

The WOUNDS are where light comes. The ex-scapegoat is brimming with this light and wisdom.

Being a constant pin cushion is a wretched role for a child but greatness is the end result.

DYSFUNCTIONAL FAMILY TRAITS

A healthy system encourages all members to be seen, heard and validated without fear of rejection.

As the dysfunctional parent projected her crap onto the one, the others joined in on the fun.

In these systems abuse and neglect are permitted but it's the talking about em that's forbidden.

One parent is a codependent peacemaker, the other's a raging monster narc who can't manage anger.

Siblings fall into roles by accident: the golden child, the forgotten one, the bully, the scapegoat.

System traits: First is code of silence then add a dash of gaslighting/a teaspoon of shame in it.

This becomes a recipe for emotional trauma, abandonment and utter loyalty to the narcissist.

Triangulation is a major trait: involving a third in order to raise self-esteem, power or to dominate.

LIBERAL SHOVE DOWNS

They're all talking about you--vicious emotional vampires who get off on killing the shrew.

Millions killed thru ideology [Holocaust] then millions killed thru ideas [abortion]: teach this stuff.

I never went to a concentration camp but was put thru the ringer by liberal losers and I fear our future.

I became like a young child, so sensitive I couldn't be around anyone without feeling down.

Sudden demographic change is an assault on the political power of those who live there.

You can't hate a whole nation you gotta see it as social hypnosis, a wave taking over one generation.

I don't put up with neighbors of any sort: their projections/jealousies/what they think of me.

What you women put me thru, the fateful decisions you made on my behalf being so dumb and daft.

Narcissists complain it's all about narcissism now and that everyone's a narcissist--that's how they resist.

Strong empaths feel pain all around. The decent 50's kept this down but now they're overwhelmed.

If women can't get their father's love they're looking for love in men but can't give it, incapable of it.

IT'S NOT WOMEN BUT THE SPIRIT IN EM

It's not the women it's the spirit that's in them. The feminist spirit is an evil reversal/dungeon.

To be under control of a feminist is hell but maybe unfelt by the liberal democrat husband, till now.

LIBERAL SHOVE DOWNS

People didn't used to be so selfish, had community spirit. But now they are, so narcissists are everywhere.

The woman without her father's love turns her child into a transgender whether he likes it or not.

Listen to any conversation, there is nothing. We're in a **DROUGHT** of intellect and spiritual visions.

The mother was darkness. On his deathbed dad became the light separating me from her madness.

When we die there'll be no memory of the dyads, triads, interlocking jealousy patterns, birth order, etc.

The lady said "I don't blame em for hating me but it was a fatal mental illness and I was in denial you see"

Have confidence in your early works tho' you haven't reviewed them since, it's part of your dance.

YOUTHFUL PASSIONS MISDIRECTED

I was very immature and felt passionately about various things but then it all reversed with aging.

Just because we love/adore our president doesn't mean it's a Hitler situation but so thinks women.

If they think they can intimidate us with hidden threats someday we'll shut their mouths. Goebbels

A woman without her father's love and example has porous boundaries/behaves badly.

The regressive gene [gutter inferiority] only comes out through sins of which there are so many.

The flip side with repentance brings out glory, exaltedness, genius, creativity and being Godly.

LIBERAL SHOVE DOWNS

Things we take so seriously in our narcissistic jealousy triangles--all the details--die with our death.

Yes it's an amazing miracle as the jigsaw puzzle comes together as if it were planned--imagine that.

You've seen me at my most maudlin all-confessing twists and turns but now it's all done: completion.

Thank you for being my friend there, in whatever part you played tho' it coulda just been inside of me.

People who read these quips all think I'm talking about them but fear not, we're all crazy friends.

Feminist hammering is turgid and tumultuous. I got so sick of it they just won't get off of it, gosh.

UNDOING COLLEGE CULTURE

It's hard to undo college culture in your head. It may take years to re-moralize after being so misled.

Maintain your home like a movie set. Keep utter order every minute by constantly eliminating clutter.

If you start running me down after putting me high I'm not gonna take it. I'd rather be alone not adapt.

People loved dogs/cats in the 50's but never accused of having sex with them--libs have dirty minds!

You left me alone, you threw me to the wolves. Decades of dung followed carrying a torch for my foes.

I'll never forget how you sucked up to wifey's inferior views rather than the truth--pooh on you.

Yah I'm mad as hell but it built a thick shell and I'm a lot smarter than I was as a sheltered naive belle.

LIBERAL SHOVE DOWNS

Hey beta male: YOU'RE supposed to lead the family not succumb to inferior feminist narratives!

Liberals can't love cats/dogs that much due to cold hearts so they ruthlessly accuse anything novel.

A woman can lose her beauty early when God pulls the plug due to immorality and it's ugly to see.

No you can't interrupt my precious privacy to charge your phone while you sit there a total obstruction.

I can't bear the brunt of this on my shoulders anymore, that's why Jesus says on Him cast your care.

Keep putting stuff on Jesus. It's overwhelming for us to be thinking about this, He said be childlike sis.

You can be in a state of anxiety for forty years without letup--worse than war where you get R & R.

ADAPTING TO BEDLAM

Having been imposed on by groups of Millennials I'm ready for college campuses but who needs this?

Be careful with life, it can turn on a dime. Suddenly whole town hates you on a false accusation, aye.

All I can say about you is WRONG STRESSORS and frankly it's a little boring and unnerving.

Now that you're complete, return to Page. Be like Opie in wide eyed innocence but with shrewdness.

I'm so frightened of the emotional bedlam these people create I'd do ANYTHING to escape, ok?

Dear Lord I pray: They label everything the opposite to the truth so that I always end up the culprit!

LIBERAL SHOVE DOWNS

How come victims always end up as perpetrators with you? It's crazy, everything's upside down.

This is so serious being misjudged like this. It's worse than Chinese style as FB removed 22 posts.

In their presence is NOISE, nothingness, vacuity, self-centeredness, trivialities, slogans, sensuality.

An entire generation HELD BACK by cell phones constantly interrupting: this is so bad.

Don't call: If you and I talk simultaneously it cancels each other out and it's CHAOS. How is this progress?

God gave me escape from mundane reasonings of small towners who don't [CAN'T] understand.

The computer revolution saved me as I became renowned on a world level tho' despised by peons below.

WOMEN ARE JEALOUS

The women are so jealous they'd do anything to throw a wrench in your plans and rain on your parade.

What I had to go thru on the Potter's wheel to get to here I cannot describe but free of dross it's pure gold.

I guess we should just succumb to irrelevance and let these crazies take over but God said never.

I found ONE who loved me and he took me outa that bedlam into stability/happy homelife, see?

I can't stop the aging process, all I can do is rely on God. It's making Him happy that will protect me.

If it happened 80 years ago what makes you think it can't happen again? How can you so certain?

LIBERAL SHOVE DOWNS

Modern propaganda exhausts your critical thinking so as to annihilate truth--
there's an emptiness in you.

Stability/happy homelife means you are now of none effect cuz I'm protected
with a locked fence.

To save the marriage from all Jezebels I had to disengage for they're
compelled to ruin it every day.

I don't even see him. All I know is he keeps my happy homelife afloat/head
above water, amen.

They've made critical thinking an exhausting battle as they hit us with lies and
deceptive prattle.

They took me down at the beginning so I had to re-find myself in the desert
wilderness of bewildering.

All I want is a FENCE--I told you that. Happy homelife, my routines with solitude
and we both have it.

If you will keep the invasive, officious world out I'll build you an otherworldly
castle and we'll prosper.

OVERCOMING TEMPTATION

Yah, from the first time I laid eyes on you actually. I knew then but then God
intervened and saved me.

Dear Lord I'm lucky to be alive as I look back at the vicious mob of gainsayers,
mockers, sluts and slobs.

I don't mind the beard, do what you must do to feel the manosphere, it's not
my thing dear.

All I want is provision/protection so I don't have to be part of them. As a desert
rat I learned that friend.

One works all her life on the books and someone else receives a fortune from
it tho' forsook.

LIBERAL SHOVE DOWNS

You're not so funny but you think you are so go ahead, it's a level playing field and everyone's a star, eh?

Even though you're far younger, you're just too old for me and I creepily feel like I'm with my grandfather.

I'm much healthier than when in my forties in the midst of all these social maladies from lack of knowledge.

As I start the beginning of the end as Churchill said, I look back and see these things, shocked/dismayed.

I put myself at the mercy of others, feeling no sense of self-protection from swindlers or losers.

What I had to go through to learn about people was unbelievable so heed my words/stay stable.

Love yourself cuz no one else will. I learned that in the desert wilderness and it comes in handy still.

KNOWING YOUR LIMITATIONS

I know everything about myself: What I love and what I can't stand, what's worth dying for or isn't.

Once we let each other go--pass each other by--there'll be no more coming back you know, bye bye.

I spent most of life learning of obstructions the removal of which made the rest prolific and beautiful.

I actually put myself at the mercy of the whole world which I trusted unconditionally: scary!

What was the etiology? Improper bonding? Trauma? Whatever it was it kept insidiously selecting.

They wore out my will to fight. The rage went inward and I became an invalid watching TV day and night.

LIBERAL SHOVE DOWNS

They're part of the TEAM and that means ensnared in the immoral deceptive lies, mutually affirmed.

The culture affirms them agains as the nation makes laws making sin seem as righteousness--what a mess.

The poor beta [hypnotized] male doesn't have the mental apparatus to accept all this right away sis.

Culture/disaster shock, betrayal trauma, catastrophe trauma: anything can happen in America trauma.

If your arrogance shows through how am I supposed to take that from you? No contact, whew.

I doubt you're mature enough to discount the misjudgments of naive people so I bid adieu.

TAKING ON MISJUDGMENTS TO BE LIKED

If you're gonna take on their bloody misjudgments just to be counted then I reject that/be gone now.

It's true what my aunt always said: **NO ONE WILL CARE.** Tho' a sad statement it prepares you for war.

Take the red pill and relocate. Don't hang in there, can't you see the homeless/broken in cars, aye?

The bible says the repentant see the danger and get away, the wicked hang in there anyway.

They make us crazy again by making righteousness a violation of law--land without justice that's all.

He's done looking for truth, he just manages information. There's a big difference and who can stand it?

Where ignorance is bliss it is folly to be wise. That's the culture we live in, cutting you down to size.

LIBERAL SHOVE DOWNS

They are not motivated by reason but by love of their sins. As you know they flare up over nothing it seems.

You must conform exactly to what they're saying or you're on the other side and they're complaining.

Identity politics is the politics of our time, the refuge of the scoundrel and blind boastful twitter hater.

If they make a mistake I don't want them punished with a baby. Barrack Obama

Invaded by kids born in the sixties and man oh man did they make me crazy as I learned about boundaries.

When I think all that I went thru being looked down on, disassociated and rejected by liberals.

I didn't leave the left, the left left me. Black Pigeon

POLITICS OF IDENTITY: WHO I AM

The politics of redistribution was replaced by the politics of recognition: my identity, who I am.

To have equal outcomes you'd have to have heaviest bureaucracy possible and that means ending it all.

Querulous self-righteousness combined with refusal to look inward to motives is characteristic of this age.

80-90% of black people voted for the son of Satan twice. And you say they're victims and nice?

Obama overturned "Don't ask, don't tell" in the military and since then gays run around visibly.

Longwinded narcissist thinks his every word is gold when just by his loquacity it's all bull.

When calling someone "racist" the power lies with the accusation not the facts.

LIBERAL SHOVE DOWNS

Conservatives vs. liberals. As we toughen up they just get weaker. They can't answer questions/cheaters.

New lesson from Serena incident: You cannot criticize a prominent black person without it being "racist".

Same enemies/same friends: shifting coalitions is what makes the soaps run.

UNREPORTED BLACK-ON-BLACK VIOLENCE

Black on white violence is unreported, you don't say it. Things are building so a knock on your door, fear it.

Bible reports societies filled with monsters and freaks so evil endlessly and God said kill em all please.

These days if you're smart they'll beat you up (don't understand you) so don't expect approval til' through.

An all black school is called a prison.

America's identity went from inclusion to division: demanding respect for oneself as different.

Modern Socialism get-it: it's not for middle class but identity politics around which all else orbits.

They battle in the Oppression Olympics over which group is least privileged and aren't we sick of this?

To today's left, blindness to group identity is the ultimate sin.

In the left's destructive crater identity politics and oppression olympics spiraling is at the very center.

The left's exclusionary identity politics is ironic since their whole thing was inclusion, a big problem.

We love and trust Trump not listening to fake news chumps.

LIBERAL SHOVE DOWNS

Democratic Socialism is nothing but Socialism with a nice word in front of it. Ben Shapiro

If everyone's doing "social justice" stuff how do you stand out doing crap like that? Be unique/get clout.

Abused for years by liberals in small desert town: a nightmare against conservatives you see all around.

Buy Karen Kellock Books: Amazon. There's 10+ there: early works from 2004 and now five more, mature.

FRIGHTENING FEROCIOUS FEMINISTS

Main gist of feminism: Men and women are the same but women are better.

Wiping out all differences between men and women is a social imperative cuz One-Ism triggers feminists.

Gist: Any differences between men/women (or races) are socially constructed and therefore unjust.

Women think they're not sinners. It's all the men ya' know but they're ruined by this lack of humility, utters.

Marriages break up at 6/10ths but when I broach the subject I'm banned from list if it's filled with feminists.

"I can't specifically say that he was one of the ones who assaulted me"--after accusing him of gang rape!

Key accuser backtracks on charges: "I don't know what he did". Another bites the dust: women are liars.

The false accusers--FEMINISTS--will soon fall flat on their face cuz the world is sick of these antics/disgrace.

I'm interested in men cuz they're different from me. How they know all about engines/tools fascinates me.

LIBERAL SHOVE DOWNS

Men are so logical and sweet--they just wanna please! But then there's the feminist/bitchy wannabes.

God purposefully put me in hard gnarly situations so I could solve them and then write all about em.

I could write about failed feminism to fill a library cuz I had two older feminist sisters tyrannizing over me.

My mother gave up her morals and religion to maintain relationship with my sisters: liberals and fems.

To be in conflict between right and fitting the blight she had to drink, daily-- that was the secondary tragedy.

LOVING THE WHOLE WORLD OR SLUR

From resisting losing her culture she "loved the whole world" then got drunk daily to submerge the slur.

Liberal feminists hate the conservative lady in their family. She puts everything they think crazily in jeopardy.

Women were supposed to take care of the children or write hymns not preach fem/Jezebel doctrines.

Jezebel is man-hating (makes em into wimps with bickering) and that's why it hates Trump, rebelling.

When women exit the haze of Jezebel Feminism they think the opposite to everything they did.

Most of the problems we have to day are created by optimists.

6500 genetic differences between men and women--how could anyone say they are the same or even similar?

Stay away from me you grabby, gabby Jezebel.

Men and women are the same: all differences are socially constructed and need to be wiped out/tamed.

LIBERAL SHOVE DOWNS

He-she wrestler beat female opponent so bad her career ended--and we're supposed to be ok with this.

They say there's no binary since there are intersex people. Deconstruct: This is all political to screw us up.

Non-binary is anti-male just as diversity is anti-white.

NON-BINARY IS ANTI-MALE

There were a few good members but basically run by females and they were uncaring, vapid, tough, cruel.

Be under a woman tyrant and you'll wish it was a man cuz they've had centuries to temper power man.

Women are choosing to raise children without fathers. Of course, men in general are shoved asunder.

Violent, alcoholic and schooled in psychological terror she sure doesn't seem to be a natural mother.

Good housekeepers are "obsessive compulsive"--beginning with Harriet Craig (1949) movie brainwashing this.

Jezebel: Given a chance she'll take your stuff, your boyfriend, your friends and your good reputation.

Men are so much better at being female athletes. And beating them--in fact they knock em out/cheat.

She smashed her racquet on the court but she had many cuz they're used to this kinda crap of course.

See what liberal feminism does? She'll go down in history as a crazy feminist/tennis genius.

"You owe me an apology—say you're sorry" wow we're really seeing 30s-something immaturity.

LIBERAL SHOVE DOWNS

For years she thought she was supposed to be angry all the time--her favorite phrase was "I'm furious".

"If I could I would take this f-ing ball and shove it down your f-ing throat". Serena Williams to linesman.

"Men do things much worse than that--this is not fair". Wow, I've heard that before from the immature.

"Other people were speeding too, officer" yah but you were the one pulled over.

WOMEN'S RIGHTS AND ALL KINDS OF STUFF

After throwing an ugly tirade "I'm here fighting for women's rights, equality and all kinds of stuff". Yuk

Fight for women's rights by refusing to be subject to the rules they agreed to, yah that's them alright.

Women's Rights: The right to not be subject to the rules you agreed to.

A "feminist" who has been incredibly cruel to other women in the sport.

You must push back against verbal abuse of judges because if it ever worked it would escalate with jerks.

Serena to the linesman: "Are you the one who screwed me over last time? You're ugly on the inside".

Saying "those shouldn't be the rules" doesn't change the rules. That's why you're paid millions, fools.

Which proves being filthy rich with millions of fans doesn't make you a mature or even a nice woman.

It will come out--your immaturities will be shouted from the rooftops!

PRO TENNIS CHANGES AS FEMINISM DERANGES IT

Female empowerment apparently means not having to play by the rules you agreed to.

LIBERAL SHOVE DOWNS

Men have to play five sets, women only three. But they got equal pay anyway, for 60% of the work, see?

Women size each other up and bash em down. Don't discuss your plans with em it's only God's plan.

Men have learned thru the centuries how to temper power, keep their enemies closer or transmute fear.

How can you watch NFL when you have Women's Tennis, the real sport of men?

Now is the time for the fake feminist showdown. Women have it all wrong and men must now show them.

The linesman didn't "steal a point from her" but made her accountable for her actions.

To not criticize Serena Williams because she has ovaries and dark skin is the very definition of sexism.

Lord, how long will the wicked triumph and exult? Psalms 94: 3

Men are so much better at tennis it isn't funny yet the media says that's a sexist comment/can't face reality.

Two feminist sisters who totally rejected me/conservatism as stated here and thus my drive to be up there.

HEAVENLY HOME OR ANGRY FEMINIST SLUM?

A loving home is a touch of heaven until degraded into hellhole sewer by feminist leaven.

Women are supposed to be keepers of the hearth, to hold things high and keep the bad out, bye bye.

They're so sweet when they go off to college but then arrogance takes over and a Jezebel Spirit/deranged.

LIBERAL SHOVE DOWNS

It wasn't a temperment breakdown/disgustingly infantile reaction it was "fighting for women's rights".

Yes she abused her racquet but Ramos abused his authority. Women's Tennis Association Racket

Modernization of sports replaced the classical notion of "virtue" with the modern one of political correctness.

They now use sport to promote feminism, multiculturalism, ethno-nationalism or sexual identity.

The stellar virtue of classical athleticism is now replaced by the pseudo virtue of victimization.

PATHETICALLY INFANTILE BEHAVIOR IS V ALOR

Pathetically infantile behavior is now transformed into the greatest valor.

An embarrassing adult temper tantrum is all-ok if it stands up for political correctness.

Instead of promoting virtue/self-control their sport's used for feminism, multiculturalism, sex identity.

So-called virtue of feminist-inspired equal rights justifies acting out in the most absurd tantrums/fights.

Having been placed in absurd liberal feminist drunken environment I built muscle/could write about it.

Serena Williams meltdown is a public demonstration of just how morally vapid political correctness is.

Naomi is the true champion, showing respect for her opponent while her opponent only herself.

The 3 R's: Rights, Respect and Responsibility means filthy pornographic Sex Ed starting in kindergarden.

LIBERAL SHOVE DOWNS

"Gender expression" is one thing: fashion. It's how you present yourself in public not victimization.

So now fashion-criticism will be a hate crime.

With millions riding on the game you think judge-abuse is rare? They gotta be strong/ignore the dare.

Women should be able to break all the rules they themselves agreed to. This is all bull/ typical of females.

When the richest most powerful athlete has a tantrum it looks to them instead like obvious racism/sexism.

Incredibly but predictably the lilberal women are bedding down migrants. No kidding, this is serious.

WOMEN HOLD EACH OTHER DOWN

Women hold each other down like crabs in a bucket and I'm telling you I'm sick of it. Ignore em/fu**it.

Fat women, dumb women, dumpy/old women are bedding down migrants who are happy to oblige em.

Once the evil Jezebel spirit is gone thru knowledge alone everything comes into divine order once again.

Loving home is a touch of heaven but when it's leaven and feminists dominatin' it's a hellhole of shoutin'.

Dumpy middle aged women having sex with handsome migrants who can see thru em and are using em.

It was so horrible to be under a liberal feminist I can't even describe it: the illogical flipflops/I defied it.

Pocahontus Fullashit continued liberal tradition of <u>just making it up</u> for Harvard University professorship.

A good housekeeper is thorough: behind and under!

LIBERAL SHOVE DOWNS

Migrants have become boy toys for leftist menopausal women? Yes sir and they'll even travel for it.

Women act like crabs in a bucket when they get with each other so just walk away even if it's mother.

You don't respond with joy just because you can't handle negativity in your life.

JOY AND LOVE NO MATTER THE FACTS

Anger and resentment can be Defending Moral Values and love and forgiveness don't belong here Sue.

Since they can't handle negativity everything is good. It's all virtue signaling but through hearts of wood.

It's not men holding women down! Like crabs in a barrel they do that themselves and it's cruel.

Women think "love and kindness"--not truth--comes first. Would kindness with Hitler have worked?

Middle aged liberal women are bedding down migrants and that's a fact overlooked about sluts.

Virtue signaling, kindness without repentance and other women tendencies have cruel outcomes believe me.

Many of the "champions" self-indulge in virtue signaling to distract from their poor performances.

Crazy women forcing veganism on their poor dogs, cats and children--all because they "love them".

Radical feminists have lost the plot. They are very pugnacious, heck in the 80's they were beating me up. Start

I revel in being a woman as that's what God has assigned me--tho' logical it's the humble feminine.

LIBERAL SHOVE DOWNS

The price of endlessly appealing to female vanity is anti-male sentiment. Stefan Molyneux

I hereby will not talk, discuss or argue with liberal feminists ever again cuz as long as they're one it's sin.

A crappy mother relationship ruins your life but God gives another chance: forgive her/no more strife.

VIRTUE SIGNALING CREATES TRAGEDY

Here I was, an anchor in the mud for my sister's virtue signaling and it lasted for years: my neurotic tragedy.

The daughter was unconsciously being used to dampen the Nazi guilt of the parent, also abused.

Two lesbians who had a son who turned out to be trans, oh what a surprise.

A simple reprimand becomes bullying or misogyny with feminist babies.

Serena took the two components of identity politics: black and female. An atom bomb but she still lost/failed.

PULLING THE FEMALE CARD

Pulled the female card and cried on the court, starting a social justice tirade while the crowd roared.

It's incredibly sexist and racist to excuse her bad behavior because she was black or female.

Black women lack the emotional fortitude to keep their cool in tough situations so we should pity them?

Pitying them rather than expecting better is the bigotry of low expectations-- like with Serena it ruins em.

Racquet-smashing and crying victim is fighting for women's rights.

LIBERAL SHOVE DOWNS

Most of the problems we have to day are created by optimists.
Non-binary is anti-male just as diversity is anti-white. Men turning feminine, women just bright.

I judged myself through their eyes. They saw me as insignificant, replaceable, not worth a cent.

There were a few good members but basically run by females and they were uncaring, vapid, tough, cruel.

Be under a woman tyrant and you'll wish it was a man cuz they've had centuries to temper power man.

Anything can replace anything and it will be the same. That's interchangeability, the concept of the lame.

HOSTILE INVASION OF YOUNG MEN

Why must we embrace large numbers of people so unlike ourselves? No other race is ever asked this.

They want em coming very fast in large numbers cuz that WILL bring change, not tiny groups assimilating.

Marxism and communism was done in the name of equality then hundreds of millions people were dead.

Low openness associated with high orderliness is interpreted as "disgust" and I can say that it sure is.

It's not flattering that he's whining and weeping--that's just his only way of winning so avoid him.

Repeat again: Low Openness combined with High Order equals Disgust.

They tie our hands behind our back while handing the EU a baseball bat. European citizen

It's all due to Western Ethno-Masochism: white people hating themselves. Why else care more for others?

LIBERAL SHOVE DOWNS

"Replacism" is the idea of general interchangeability: that one group equals (same as) another, unbelievably.

NWO: Motive #1 for mass immigration is dissolve nations. Motive #2: use em as social engineers for change.

The acceptance of multiculturalism means they also accept international agreements killing nationalism.

Soldiers always fought for independence and democracy by defending their borders, you don't know this?

Equality of Outcome is dangerous beyond belief. It's Robin Hood communism steal your life like a thief.

THE DEMENTED LEFT HELPS THE RICH

The demented left helps the rich with massive immigration, internationalism and multiculturalism.

Obama called written tests "racial discrimination" making it simple for foreigners to scam our great nation.

Anything can replace anything and it will be the same. That's interchangeability, the concept of the lame.

We've gotten so bad that open border politicians are actually called "centrist".

Whites have a culture, more than most. Who ever started the rumor we were boring milquetoast?

Create civil war to leave EU dictators in power/army controlling borders: Merkel's Kalergi plan of course.

McCain wanted to turn our great majority white country into just another part of the third world/shoddy.

Whoever wants open borders wants America poor. That is the socialist's plan so they promise more.

LIBERAL SHOVE DOWNS

A majority white safe place for now, but how long before we too are flooded with strangers we don't know?

200 million people into Europe in the next two decades, mostly from Africa.

Globalism is simply the extent of WWII eugenicist Nazi gone underground.

All who know the joys of freedom are winners. WWII survivor

Young male migrant pushes ahead of an old feeble woman in the food line and the state calls her a "Nazi"

First three issues of future politics: border security, economic security, cultural security—that's it.

There's nothing they can do short of war to stop the nationalist age flourishing all around us: Yes!

THE CRUELTY OF TRANSNATIONAL

Transnational dynamics encouraged mass (massive) immigration having no loyalty to local customs.

Global division of labor: Labor goes to third world and rural screwed as capital finance stays in urban areas.

Rural: Mass unemployment in globalist economies when work goes to poor countries/money goes to cities.

Cruel Events: Globalism's narcissistic/consumer based values replacing timeless customs/traditions.

Matteo Salvini: 70% approval as he gives flat tax to encourage growth and incentivizes high birth rate.

80% of central American women are raped when crossing the border. The families know it/warn her.

China (Chicoms) meddle 1000x more than Russia ever could but the liberals love them/help em.

LIBERAL SHOVE DOWNS

Anyone not for importing millions of unvetted military age men is an extremist, can't you see this?

Multiculturalism means one thing for sure: the erosion of the culture of the native people made poor.

An ivy league study shows illegal pop is 22 million--twice what they said as if we were brain dead.

In communism you don't work 8 hours a day you gotta be at work 8 hours a day producing nothing, ok?

Left has left the middle class behind who want Trump--to remedy they import new voting block.

MERKEL MADNESS SEEN AS FEMALE LOVINGNESS

Merkel madness has destroyed European culture. A merchant of misery a little lower than Uncle Hitler.

They're the shit of the earth--they barbecue live dogs, a curse--and you wanna let em all in/put em first?

It's all due to Western Ethno-Masochism: white people hating themselves. Why else care more for others?

"Replacism" is the idea of general interchangeability: that one group equals (same as) another, unbelievably.

Is it racist against blacks to say they create 500% more crimes than natives? Or immigrants, 4000% more?

Appreciation of freedom is the highest winning. Concentration camp survivor

In any discovery, you don't tell em you trigger em--to see analogies in self unseen before now.

Yellow Jacket movement in France is anti-immigration of radical Islam not the tax--that's just the straw.

It was on the horizon but now it's run us over.

LIBERAL SHOVE DOWNS

Are they gonna pull the plug, are they gonna make em leave? Cuz even if they block the flow it still stinks.

Liberalism is a mental illness characterized by lack of disgust--what would horrify most, they brush off.

How liberalism sux: they have no disgust.

LIBERALISM SUX CUZ IT HAS NO DISGUST

Big mega corporations are allied with China and the communists, radical Islam and God-hating leftists.

It was hard to admit global government was tied to radical Islam or that they were targeting our families.

Weaponized Third World Populations: Because we forced these terms, the fight is on and not just Macron.

Humanity is awakening and the process is accelerating! All over the world yellow vests are protesting.

It's **NOT** the French government but an occupation by a group of globalist dirtbags led by a pretty boy.

If a leader brings in third world pops pooping everywhere then he's no better than a traitor/collaborator.

You have battered our people, squeezed them. They have a right to revolt/we'll arrest for treason. French Generals

UN Migration Pact: Even if a country doesn't want em in, they will force them in, white dissidents arrested.

TREASON: Open borders, announce to come here everything's free then your own people raped/killed/forgotten.

The UN Migration Pact is not legally binding but greases the skids for unlimited mass third world immigration.

LIBERAL SHOVE DOWNS

Sweden has the highest crime rate in the world (whereas just ten years ago, the lowest) due to globalist traitors.

GOD LOVERS ARE GROUP HATERS

I can't go to your church, your potluck or any other group gatherings. More people = more sickening.

I hate groups with a passion. I'm reading minds, I feel the psychic dis, they're sizing me up, I'm pist.

Going to your group, adapting to your time schedules and listening to your boring words: pooh!

The chemically sensitive are shut-ins without regret cuz the world is filled with toxic poisons and s**t.

It's incredibly beneficial to see the wild wickedness of people for if you don't they'll take control.

JUNK SCIENCE AND HISTORICAL REVISIONISM

The all-forgiving enables your enemies. She/he is a Frenemy Enabler.

Junk science and historical revisionism has taken over the dumb by the clever and truth is gone forever.

If I say things you don't like that's not hate speech and if you say it is then you are a fascist. Ben Shapiro

No ambition like earlier years--we lost our lives to trivial matters while the government helped invaders.

We whites are to be remembered as slave owners, not the creators of the modern world powers.

God said: How long will you pine over people who don't care about you, or who are dead? Sail on instead.

Ben Shapiro/Jordan Peterson are whatcha call "approved opposition" while the true opposition is slammed.

LIBERAL SHOVE DOWNS

The "approved opposition" stinkers move the Overton window to the left while posing as conservatives.

The hard left Antifa set up a "near left" of fake opposition like these neoCons Ben and Jordan.

The hard SJW globalist left has always done this (create a fake right) moving the herd into the final fight.

The neoCon directives to fake opposers is far, far away from nationalism and policies for America first.

Fake posers like Shapiro are the Washington general elite to demonize truth and lead em all into defeat.

Jordan Peterson/Ben Shapiro are the Judas Goats who timid cons get behind cuz they have the votes.

Neocon fakers are there to gatekeep/mislead the right, conservatives, nationalists and Christians.

The neocon fakers are the "Ok Conservatives" and oh what a rat hole created by these commie traitors.

it's about disclaiming rather than telling us what it's about! Stop assuming we know the backdrop.

NEO-CON GLOBALIST TROJAN HORSES

The Shapiro/Petersons are created to misdirect/divide since they know the truth and numbers are on our side.

Jordan Peterson and Ben Shapiro are the "far right intellectuals" to deliver us into world government.

It's incredible how the public's in the dark about how Shapiro and Peterson are the new Trojan Horse.

Since the bible says all the nations will remain at the end, we know that globalism will fail friends.

LIBERAL SHOVE DOWNS

Happy aging (eldering) is right viewpoint: It's not the END it's the beginning of the end, the HIGHEST blend.
Saddlebags on side/top of butt: If a woman's going to eat anything of quality she'll have these bumps.

They spend all their time disclaiming bad rumors rather than just educating us/giving us the scoop!

My husband said they're sexy--defining me as a woman--but I never saw em as a malnourished vegan.

They're always rising up Jordan Petersons in order to neutralize the stronger force--US/without globalists.

Support the truth you believe in, not these fake conservatives and Judas goats leading us to destruction.

If you value your mind give yourself plenty of office time. It's all yours--from outside draw the line.

Justify all-day office time even if you just look out the window, musing. This is most worthwhile/promising.

Anti-Anglo is always dressed up as "anti-racism".

If you import the Third World you ARE making it more poor, dirty and divided but saying that gets you fired.

Is there nothing we won't put up with, with the bullying left and their cultural take-over? I wonder

DON'T TELL ME THE LIBERAL NARRATIVE I REJECT IT

Don't tell me, I know the liberal narrative: You bought it whole but the smart didn't buy it at all.

God said "I don't wantcha working during days--just the mornings then no more focus (go to right brain), ok?

There's a CLICK as you switch from left-brain to right-brain or back again. It's ACTIVE vs. RECEPTIVE.

LIBERAL SHOVE DOWNS

It's a DELIGHT to go from extreme focus (work) to relaxed/diffuse focus (relaxation and perks).

Takes me a while to relax after all that but music helps to make the switch to ECSTASY, bliss, excitement.

That's what you wanna believe but it's not science at all. Between races and genders there's total differential.

You have to memorize this new jargon to know what the human race is all about according to these louts.

Most older people are so lonely they don't care about privacy but boy that's not me, I want more each day.

Telling people about the historic world-altering achievements of white men can get you sent to prison.

Pride for your white race is now stigmatized by liberals, the media and establishment as a whole.

Every other race without exception is allowed to be proud but not us, that's a sing of your horribleness.

The narrative: white Europeans are the bad guys and everyone else must unite to cut em down to size.

Saying "merry Christmas" is so insensitive and divisive--said by mean generation throwbacks.

EQUALITY OF OUTCOME IS HORRIBLE

Leftist ideology is based on equality of outcome not equality of opportunity= Communism/unfree.

Society that puts equality ahead of freedom will end up with neither but put freedom first, *both*.

LIBERAL SHOVE DOWNS

"Inequality is evil" so different outcomes can *only* mean something unjust has happened?

I know what it's like people moving in on you and whether town or block it's hell on earth too.

We just want our own lives or there's weird stuff happening, outa control, exasperating.

Parallel societies, political Islam and radicalization have no place in our country. Sebastian Kurz

All across Europe they're reversing the demographic decline by having babies, lots of em, oh my.

Conservative traditionalists are having children while liberal globalists aren't so it's turning around.

Spain will wake up but a huge price to pay as these incompatible people cause trouble, ok?

Spain, there's only one solution: they gotta go back!

The pathological altruism of immature kids says "we need more migrants" feeling so sorry for em.

MERKEL MADNESS AND FEMALE ILLOGIC/VIRTUE SIGNALING

"We need new blood to fund pensions" but they go right on the dole, taxpayers fund em.

Migrants: They don't fund the system they suck off the system.

Anyone who hasn't come into contact with em has no idea what they're like, esp. those from Africa.

Red carpet glamour after spouting fibbers without suffering consequences of open borders.

They seem fresh and innovative but their ideas are destructive and old, socialism is cold.

LIBERAL SHOVE DOWNS

Innocent German people were punished twice: once by Hitler then Merkel and her open borders.

Merkel, the Chancellor of Open Borders has embraced the evil policies of the far-left dreamers.

Crazy socialist Merkel let a flood into small bucolic towns. Preposterous, evil, shut her down!

Her two experiments--open borders and green energy--enriched her friends with halos immense.

"We need new blood to fund pensions" but they go right on the dole, taxpayers fund em.

"No more power without accountability--you've met your match in Donald Trump" Nigel Farage

Mrs. Mae we did not vote for a transition but to instantly leave the EU organization. Nigel Farage

BBC has been encrypted into the globalist cause so we're down on them too as fake news.

When Europeans realize a picture of dead child doesn't mean to destroy their societies, Soros dies.

For Hitler it was an ideological crusade worth the sacrifice of millions of lives and it's similar today.

PEOPLE SEEN AS STATISTICS NOT RAW FACTS

The whole world should be able to come here supported by you and anything less is racism.

ICE: Those who enforce the law are criminals and the real criminals are new American citizens?

War is peace, freedom is slavery, ignorance is strength. George Orwell

LIBERAL SHOVE DOWNS

Today if you don't want immigrants flooding your country you are racist by default/you're kicked out.

It's "IN" to be poor/austere cuz the globalists want you under their thumb, it's called Feudalism.

EU heads the richest on earth but wants you poor so they make even more as immigration soars.

It's a military invasion disguised as a migrant refugee crisis so gear up/get ready.

When the facts make blacks or Hispanics look bad you don't say it--now you know the facts.

No sane country lets millions of foreigners in to put their snouts in the public trough. Jarad Taylor

When enough people get angry things change.

As illegals pile up on the border the dems insist on letting em all along with those who keep comin'.

Unskilled, uncultured, unwanted. Liberals wanna change all that and make em top of the pack.

The nasty EU stands for "tolerance, diversity and human rights" and we are rejecting them all.

Matteo Salvini knows they're trying to flood Europe with illegal migrants funded by troublemakers.

Low IQ pops propagate the spread of infectious diseases. Eppig 2010

WE'RE ON THE PATH OF SOUTH AFRICA

We're on path of South Africa with irrevocable snowball of black on white violence, God help us.

Whites are the most accepting/tolerant in the world. No other race accepts floods of foreigners.

LIBERAL SHOVE DOWNS

Cultures vary on callousness vs. sensitivity. Whites always escape when non-whites rule visibly.

Kill whitey race baiting is now merging with Islam and gangster culture, all socially engineered.

Diversity means: fewer white people. How could anyone celebrate their declining influence?

Whites letting others become a dominant force in their country is a virtuous and good thing?

They come in boats: low IQ pops. To the white men they say: "shut up, pay the bills and die off".

An unarmed invasion brings the same as an armed one: loss of land, language, culture, mind.

We don't want foreigners waltzing into our country and going on the public dole. Jared Taylor

The entire mission of the children of the lie is to lower the percentage of whites in our country.

The people they're bringing in are socialist, communist, without values and used to s-holes.

When people of color take over America it's done, over.

NASTINESS AND DISRESPECT

Look at the violence, the lack of respect, the nastiness, the dirtiness and ghettos brought to us.

White Americans created the greatest country this side of heaven and now look at Europe, it's gone.

White people in Europe don't have the freedom to disagree with the people of color, the POCs.

LIBERAL SHOVE DOWNS

White people built Europe and now POCs are there destroying it/arresting em for speaking up

The whites joined forces in America after the awful shock of the nasty evil communist Obama.

After they saw what nasty Barrack did to this great country in just 8 years they said **NEVER AGAIN.**

After that disaster they brought in a good man, a white man, a straight conservative Christian.

POCs are not happy that the whites organized and outvoted em for the good of the country.

Creeps like Maxine Waters are hellbent on bringing in POCs as they hate the Great White Hope.

Dems want these godless people here not cuz they love em but for the votes.

They seduce these pops with free stuff and setting them up to hate white people enough.

Anomalies: white authors writing "unbearable whiteness"--self-hatred you never see in other races.

It's genetic with whites to just subsume guilt and assume the whole world's problems. Gavin Mcinnes

EQUAL RIGHTS VS. "EQUALITY OF OUTCOME"

Equal rights is vastly different from "equality of outcome" which is deadly and dangerous.

We want borders/see immigrants as the problem, they want immigrants, borders are the problem.

They're taught by way of apps and leaflets how to lie when they get here and move us all out.

LIBERAL SHOVE DOWNS

Logic: Can't take care of both immigrants AND citizens and Salvini's answered that contradiction.

With illegal immigration they're shown by way of apps how to beat the system to our disadvantage.

The more immigration the less tolerance. Diversity does not increase it as the liberals insist.

Globalism makes all borders irrelevant.

Accepting more invaders is the road to hell for Europe. Czech PM

For thousands of years immigrants adapted to the host but now the host must adapt to immigrants.

Since globalization is transcultural, states must adapt to immigration "make em welcome".

They wanna go home anyway so pull the plug and they'll leave, vamoose, disappear, hurray!

All across Europe is a revitalization of classical greatness as well as what Christianity really means.

Fake news is trying to destroy America and are the friends of our enemies the globalists, you betcha.

Politicians protect guilty for votes and police are so afraid of being branded racist you know.

MULTICULTURALISTS STONING RAPED WOMEN

Multiculturalists accept stoning for raped women. You accept all cultures, right, vermin?

Barrack knew exactly what he was doing destroying America for he's not a dumb man just barbaric.

Venezuelan socialism: Water, water everywhere but not a drop to drink.

LIBERAL SHOVE DOWNS

Shunned from the center we got stronger on the periphery as we worked on ourselves and waited.

Europe is being invaded and they are allowing it to happen. We are next unless a quick turnaround.

Help individual refugees, yes. But floods coming here, no thanks!

Virtue signaling and feeling good about herself is more important than possibly millions killed.

Such jubilation--what are they fleeing from? Not having to work--they've been promised millions.

We don't believe the argument anymore that mass migration is needed due to emergency. Viktor Orban

Italy's new populist government's euroskepticism has alarmed Brussels, good we don't need em.

The Renaissance and the Enlightenment were derived from Christian European culture in sum.

It's not about left vs. right but left vs. west.

YOUR SOLUTION: GET TO WORK--DISCOVERY!

I make em mad to make em think. It's in brutal reversals from their ordinary mundane world, rinky-dink

In this generation we're expected to be social not independent. Get offa my back--I'll do what I want!

Glad to be banned from facebook, first time in ten years I've had a break and my absence may sell books.

You're done, let it go, you're now in retirement. Get beyond it, disown it knowing angels will perfect it.

Let God be your Promoter and wait to be discovered.

LIBERAL SHOVE DOWNS

Criticism of mass immigration is banned as hate speech but it's really about silencing opposition.

I've just been doing the keywords and descriptions cuz that's what draws em in through search engines.

I'm just doing the FRAME now. Correct and firm, correct and firm while always seeing the whole.

The most important books are Contagion of Madness, Supercilious and E-race White--occurring overnight.

How to be a millionaire: Once you see how it works with little, expand it forever then enjoy the boss chair.

DO THE WORK, DESERVE SUCCESS

Once you believe a lie you cannot believe the truth. Only angry people believe lies/entire cultures too.

Gaslighting: "Just cuz you perceive it doesn't make it true"—they question our senses about this big mess.

You may pay in your forties for what you did in your twenties since God doesn't always punish speedily.

After completion of the Creative Act the holy sage returns to stillness and just a page not a royal highness.

Come up with twenty titles, paste on completed work. Put all files in a folder and give to helper.

Parody: exaggerate it [hyperbolic] then they say "yes he IS like that" and he's blamed for all of it.

Just a page, a child: Enjoying each moment without any more deadlines or urgent need for approval.

I get it--you have to give the books away first, make a name/fanbase then pull the plug on free stuff.

LIBERAL SHOVE DOWNS

You will be constantly getting new ideas but the trick is, how do you store them? Be an organizational genius.

100 KAREN KELLOCK BOOKS

AFFINITY OR MISERY
AGELESS CORNUCOPIA
AMERICA AWAKE!
AMERICA'S DAFT ERA
ARTS OF PALEO FASTING
AUTOPHAGY ON CHEATERS
BACKSTABBING NEUROTICS
BETRAYAL TRAUMA
BOOMERS AND BROKENNESS
BOOT ON NECK
CHAMPION GUIDES
COMMIE NUTHOUSE
COMMIES
COMMUNIST SPIRIT
CONTAGION OF MADNESS
CONTAGIOUS MADNESS
CULTURE CLASH BASHED
DAFT LEFT
DAILY FASTARIAN
DAM RATS
DIVERSITY IS CRUELTY
E-RACE WHITE
EVIL FREAKS (Beyond Gross)
THE END OR A BEND?
FEMALE BULLIES AND FEMI-NAZIS
FEMALE CARNALITY
FEMALE DUMB DOWN
FEMALE POWER DRIVE
FEMINISM AND RUIN 1 & 2
FIX FOR MISFITS
FOOLS & TRAMPS
FREEDOM SPEAKING
FRENEMY ENABLER
FRENEMY LIAR
FRENEMY THIEF
FRENEMY TRAITOR
TRENEMY TYRANT
GENIUS IS HELD DOWN
GLOBALISLAM
GOD USES THE FLAWED
HAZE OF THE LATTER DAYS

KAREN KELLOCK PH.D.

M.S. Political Science, San Diego State. Ph.D. in Psychology, University of California Irvine. Postdoctoral: UCI School of Medicine, Dept. of Psychiatry [NIMH Grants]. Developed the Debris Theory of Disease, a theory of system pathology in 120 books and 22 textbooks for the general public. The theory has a general formula: All disease is obstruction, all recovery is elimination, all success is attraction. The three obstructions are people, habit and food. Remove obstruction and snap to your goals, waiting in the wings.